GREATEST WARRIORS
PIRATES

ALEX STEWART

ARCTURUS

This edition first published in 2014 by Arcturus Publishing

Distributed by Black Rabbit Books
P.O. Box 3263
Mankato
Minnesota MN 56002

Edited and designed by: Discovery Books Ltd.

Library of Congress Cataloging-in-Publication Data

Stewart, Alex, 1950-
 Pirates / Alex Stewart.
    pages cm. -- (Greatest warriors)
 Includes index.
 Summary: "Provides young readers with exciting details, facts, and statistics about historical pirates"--Provided by publisher.
 Audience: Grades 4-6.
 ISBN 978-1-78212-401-6 (library binding)
 1. Pirates--Juvenile literature. I. Title.
 G535.S818 2014
 910.4'5--dc23

                          2013005700

Series concept: Joe Harris
Managing editor for Discovery Books: Laura Durman
Editor: Clare Collinson
Picture researcher: Clare Collinson
Designer: Ian Winton

Picture credits:
Alamy: p. 10 (Moviestore collection Ltd), p. 17 (Adrian Buck), pp. 20, 21 (AF archive), p. 23 (RIA Novosti), p. 24 (E. Katie Holm), p. 25 (Lebrecht Music and Arts Photo Library); Corbis: p. 6 (JP Laffont/Sygma), p. 27 (Joel W. Rogers); Getty Images: pp. 9, 22 (Candela Foto Art/Kreuziger), p. 19 (Syfy); iStockphoto.com: p. 11l (davidf), p. 15 (carrollphoto); Photoshot: p. 26 (Band Photo/ uppa.co.uk), p. 29 (Idols); Rex Features: p. 4 (Everett Collection), p. 12 (c.W.Disney/Everett); Shutterstock Images: title (Tom Antos), p. 5 (Paul McKinnon), p. 7l (Bronskov), p. 7r (Myotis), p. 8 (Richard Welter), p. 11r (StacieStauffSmith Photos), p. 14l (pzAxe), p. 14r (Horimono), p. 16 (RCPPHOTO), p. 18t (Mariano Heluani), p. 18b (Pres Panayotov), p. 28 (yuanann); Wikimedia Commons: p. 13. Cover images: Getty Images: top (Candela Foto Art/Kreuziger); iStockphoto.com: bottom centre (davidf); Shutterstock Images: background (Patryk Kosmider).

Printed in China

SL002667US
Supplier 03, Date 0513, Print Run 2358

CONTENTS

ROBBERS OF THE SEA

Pirates! The word sent terror through the heart of every sailor that ever went to sea. From ancient times, pirates attacked and **plundered** ships in all the world's oceans. They took whatever they found, from gold to slaves, and often killed those who got in their way.

SEA THIEF

Pirates were tough and ruthless seafarers who chose a life of battles and adventure on the high seas in the hope of becoming rich.

FIGHTING TALK

Buccaneers, corsairs, and privateers

The word *pirate* refers to all sea robbers, but there were several different types of pirate. Buccaneers were pirates operating in the Caribbean Sea in the seventeenth century. Corsairs attacked shipping in the southern Mediterranean, often from bases on the Barbary Coast in North Africa. Privateers had permission from their government to seize ships and **cargo** from enemy nations. Privateers were seen as heroes at home, but victims saw them as pirates.

TREASURE HUNTERS

Ever since **traders** sailed the seas, pirates preyed on their **vessels**. Over 2,500 years ago, pirates used fast warships called **biremes** to steal precious cargo from ancient Greek **merchant ships**. In Roman times, pirates stole valuable olive oil and grain, and took captives to sell as slaves. In the sixteenth century, ships bringing treasure from the Americas to Europe gave pirates rich and tempting new targets.

PIRATE SHIP

From the sixteenth century, pirates often converted merchant ships, similar to this replica of the eighteenth-century HMS *Bounty*, into warships by equipping them with extra cannon.

PIRATES OF THE GOLDEN AGE

In the sixteenth century, Spain conquered a vast empire in South and Central America. Soon, Spanish galleons began to bring vast quantities of gold and silver back to Europe. The vessels, laden with treasure, were easy targets for pirates, and the "Golden Age of Piracy" began!

FORTUNE HUNTERS

Life on board a trading ship was often harsh, and conditions and pay were poor. During the Golden Age of Piracy, many merchant seamen chose a life of adventure and piracy on the high seas instead.

BAREFOOT PIRATE

In warm climates, pirates and sailors often went barefoot on the ship. This made it easier to climb the **rigging** to adjust the sails.

TELESCOPE

The telescope was a vital piece of equipment when it came to deciding whether or not a nearby ship was worth attacking.

SPANISH TREASURE

In 1545 and 1546, Spanish conquerors found gold and silver mines in South America and Mexico. On its way back to Spain, the precious metal had to pass by the Caribbean islands of Jamaica, Barbados, and Hispaniola. Here, nests of pirates lay in wait.

PIECES OF EIGHT

During the 1590s, Spain shipped nearly 7 million pounds (3 million kg) of silver and gold out of South America. Much of this **loot** was in the form of coins, such as silver dollars and gold **doubloons**. Silver dollars were known as "**pieces of eight**," because each was worth one-eighth of a Spanish dollar.

PRECIOUS CHEST

Sometimes pirates got lucky and captured a ship transporting chests of gold and silver coins.

BATTLE REPORT

HMS *Scarborough* vs. John Martel

Captain John Martel was one of the most ruthless pirates in the Caribbean in the early eighteenth century. He plundered vessels off the coast of Jamaica and is said to have killed all the sailors aboard one ship he preyed on. In 1717, a 30-gun British warship, the HMS *Scarborough*, finally trapped Martel and his ship near the island of Santa Cruz. Martel set fire to his ship rather than let it be captured. He then managed to escape and was never seen again.

BLOODY BUCCANEERS

In the seventeenth century, most of the buccaneers preying on Spanish ships in the Caribbean were British, French, or Dutch. Hoping to become rich from stolen treasure, they set up pirate bases on the islands of Tortuga and Jamaica.

PIRATES' PRIZE

From their coastal strongholds, buccaneers had clear views of the open sea and the vessels upon it. When a treasure ship came near, they sailed out to capture their prize.

PIRATES OF PORT ROYAL

Of all the pirate bases in the Caribbean, Port Royal was the most famous. The English captured the island of Jamaica from the Spanish in 1655. To defend it, the English government invited buccaneers, known as the "Brethren of the Coast," to settle in its capital, Port Royal. By the 1680s, over 6,000 people lived there, and some 200 ships visited each year. The town swarmed with **bandits**, and its pubs did a roaring trade as pirates spent their **ill-gotten** loot.

FIGHTING TALK

Henry Morgan—the swashbuckling knight

Sir Henry Morgan was the most famous of all buccaneers in Port Royal. He served in the British Royal Navy before becoming a successful privateer, preying on Spanish ships during England's war with Spain. In 1671, with over 1,000 men, he attacked the Spanish city of Panama in Central America. He captured over 400,000 pieces of eight, and the city was destroyed by fire. England had made peace with Spain in 1670, so Morgan was arrested for his illegal raid. However, instead of punishment, he was given a knighthood by King Charles II!

TRICKS AND TERROR

With pirates, there was **no such thing as a fair fight**. They used every possible trick to seize a ship and win their prize. The most important **tactic** in a pirate attack was surprise. The second was to scare the victim into handing over the loot.

SURPRISE!

Pirates planned their attacks carefully, so they could take their victims by surprise. Sometimes they flew the same flag as their prey, pretending to be from the same nation. They often disguised their ships as innocent merchant vessels by **camouflaging** their **gun ports**. In this way, they could approach their target before throwing off their disguise and attacking.

PIRATES IN HIDING

Pirates often lurked in narrow inlets along rocky shores before attacking an unsuspecting vessel.

TERROR AND THREATS

When it was too late for a target vessel to get away, pirates would hoist the pirate flag—known as the Jolly Roger. Many sailors would surrender as soon as they saw the terrifying flag. Once aboard their prey, pirates often threatened violence to make their victims hand over anything of value.

THE JOLLY ROGER

Pirates often flew plain black flags, but the Jolly Roger was sometimes black and white, marked with a frightening image such as a skull and crossed bones or swords.

YOUR JEWELS OR YOUR FINGERS!

To get their captives' rings, some pirates threatened to cut off victims' fingers!

FIGHTING TALK

The gentleman pirate

Pirates' tactics were not always successful. Stede Bonnet, also known as "the gentleman pirate" because of his family's wealth, was caught by his own tactic of hiding his ship up rivers. In 1718, Colonel William Rhett cornered Bonnet in the Cape Fear River, captured him, and handed him over to the law for **execution**.

BLACKBEARD

No pirate was more feared than Edward Teach, also known as Blackbeard. From 1716 until his death in 1718, this notorious pirate terrorized merchant seamen in the Caribbean and along the east coast of the United States.

BLACKBEARD'S FLEET

Blackbeard was an English privateer who joined a group of Caribbean pirates in 1716. By 1718, he commanded his own 40-gun warship, the *Queen Anne's Revenge*, and eight other ships. With nine ships in his fleet, he had his own small navy!

TERROR OF THE SEAS

For two long years, Blackbeard, played here by Ian McShane in the movie *Pirates of the Caribbean: On Stranger Tides*, struck terror in the hearts of innocent sailors. Most of his victims surrendered at the sight of his flag!

FEARSOME APPEARANCE

Blackbeard worked hard to create a terrifying image. He had a long, thick, black beard, which he is said to have twisted into pigtails and tied with colored ribbons. According to some accounts, before battle, he tucked slow-burning fuses under his hat, so smoke would swirl up around his face.

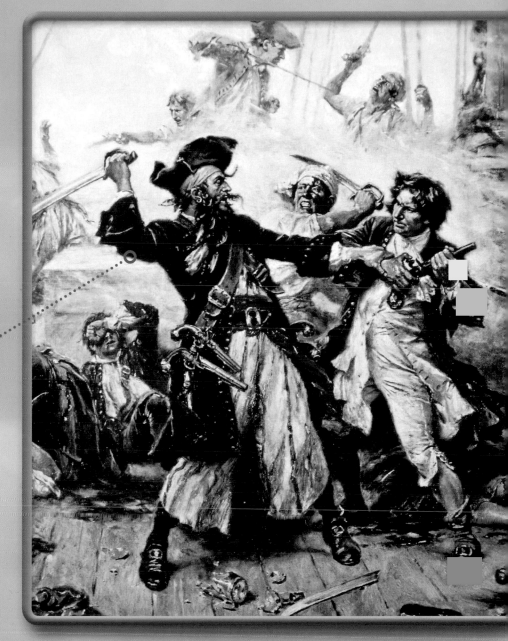

BLACKBEARD VS. LIEUTENANT MAYNARD

In this painting by Jean Leon Jerome Ferris (1920), Blackbeard is seen fighting in his last-ever battle, with Lieutenant Robert Maynard. Blackbeard was killed, and his head was hung up for all to see.

BATTLE REPORT

Battle of Ocracoke Bay, 1718

In 1718, Blackbeard was cornered off the coast of North Carolina by Lieutenant Robert Maynard of the Royal Navy. A fierce hand-to-hand battle was fought. Wielding his **cutlass**, Blackbeard broke Maynard's sword but was slashed across the neck by one of Maynard's men. Blackbeard fought on until, wounded 25 times, he eventually fell down dead. His reign of terror was over.

ARMED TO THE TEETH

To capture a ship, pirates needed to have deadly handheld weapons, so they armed themselves with the best they could steal. These included daggers, knives, swords, and cutlasses, as well as **pistols** and **muskets**.

ARMED FOR ATTACK

Pirates often carried a variety of weapons into battle. They used them to defend themselves as well as to fight for their prize.

FLINTLOCK PISTOL

Flintlock pistols were among the most valued of all pirate weapons. Their small size and light weight meant they could easily be carried when boarding a ship.

FIGHTING TALK

Flintlocks

Pirate pistols and muskets were flintlocks. Pulling the **trigger** hit a splinter of flint against a piece of steel. This caused a shower of sparks that lit gunpowder in a "pan"—creating a "flash in the pan." This set off the main charge that drove the bullet out of the barrel. Reloading was time-consuming, so pirates often carried several pistols and other weapons. It is said that Blackbeard carried six pistols tied to his belt.

14

SWORD SHAPES

Many pirates were very skilled swordsmen. They used various types of swords. The **rapier** had a long, thin blade with a lethally sharp point. It was designed for stabbing. The cutlass had a heavier, curved blade, designed for cutting and slashing.

SWORD FIGHT

This pirate has a rapier in his right hand and an ordinary sword in the left. If his slender rapier breaks, he can continue with the shorter, heavier weapon.

SHIP AHOY!

From ancient biremes powered by oars, to well-armed warships driven by the wind, pirate vessels needed to be fast and sturdy. In the Golden Age of Piracy, many pirate ships were captive merchant vessels converted for war.

PRIZED WARSHIP
From the sixteenth century, **frigates** were one of the most prized pirate ships. These warships were built for speed and could carry 40 cannon and 250 crew.

MAST
Frigates had three masts, each with several sails attached.

SAILS
The sails on some large frigates weighed up to 22,000 pounds (10,000 kg) and had a total area of 10,000 square yards (8,000 sq m).

YARD
Yards were wooden poles from which the sails were suspended. They were fixed horizontally to the masts.

RIGGING
The ropes that formed the ship's rigging were used to support the masts and control the sails.

TRADING UP

Pirate captains often started off in small ships, then traded up to larger and more powerful vessels as they became more successful. They often converted the ships they seized to make them more suitable for piracy, for instance, by removing cabins to make more room for cannon.

STEADY AS SHE GOES!

On board a pirate ship, the helmsman, or pilot, was in charge of the steering. He worked closely with the **navigator** and lookout. Dozens of men, over 100 on large vessels, were also needed for tasks such as raising and lowering the sails and anchor.

COMBAT STATS

Queen Anne's Revenge—Blackbeard's flagship

- **Type of vessel:** frigate
- **Original name:** *Concord*
- **Length:** about 90 feet (27 m)
- **Width:** about 25 feet (8 m)
- **Weight:** 660,000 pounds (300,000 kg)
- **No of masts:** 3
- **Crew:** up to 250 pirates on board
- **Guns:** 40 cannon

TAKE AIM ... FIRE!

The cannon was the pirate's deadliest weapon. The largest cannon, the demi-cannon, weighed 3,400 pounds (1,500 kg) and could fire a lead ball straight through the side of a ship. The smallest, called 2-pounders, weighed 600 pounds (270 kg) and could kill two men with a 2-pound (1-kg) shot.

WHEELED CARRIAGE
Big cannon like this weighed as much as 3,300 pounds (1,500 kg)! They were put on wheeled carriages, so they could be rolled forward for firing in battle.

CONVERTED FOR BATTLE

When pirates captured a merchant vessel, they would often convert it for their own use by cutting rows of gun ports in the hull and equipping it with cannon. This meant they were more heavily armed than most of their opponents.

GUN PORT
As well as those on the upper decks, cannon were also kept on lower decks. These helped prevent the ship from capsizing. The guns were positioned behind gun ports, which were opened for battle.

CANNON FODDER

As well as round lead balls that could smash through a ship's **hull**, cannon could be loaded with all kinds of **missiles**. Two cannon balls joined together with a chain were good for smashing rigging. Grape shot (small iron balls packed in bags) was effective against people at close range. Canister shot (lead or iron balls, gravel, and nails in a metal container) was even more deadly. Sangrenel (cloth bags full of jagged pieces of metal) produced a cloud of flying metal that could inflict horrible wounds.

CANNON CREW

It took at least three men to load and fire most cannon.

COMBAT STATS

The 32-pounder
- **Diameter of barrel:** 5 inches (130 mm)
- **Weight of shot:** 32 pounds (14.5 kg)
- **Weight of gunpowder needed to fire:** 18 pounds (8 kg)
- **Range:** 1,200 yards (1,000 m)
- **Number of men 1 shot could kill:** at least 10

The 6-pounder
- **Diameter of barrel:** 3 inches (76 mm)
- **Weight of shot:** 6 pounds (2.7 kg)
- **Weight of gunpowder needed to fire:** 6 pounds (2.7 kg)
- **Range:** 1,800 yards (1,645 m)
- **Number of men 1 shot could kill:** 3

ATTACK!

If a merchant vessel chose not to surrender when a pirate ship approached, the attack began. First came the cannon fire. Then the pirates came alongside and boarded. This is when these great warriors were at their most terrifying.

CANNON FIRE

Pirates did not generally want to sink the ships they attacked, since they hoped to steal them or their cargo. Warning shots were usually fired at first. If the victims did not surrender, the attackers then fired their cannon at the masts and rigging. Sometimes, they attacked with a "broadside"—firing all the guns on one side of their ship at the same time.

COMING ABOARD!

With the target ship disabled, the pirates sailed alongside, and armed with deadly weapons, they boarded. Some crossed on planks, some jumped, others swung into battle on ropes. Fierce hand-to-hand fighting often followed. Brave merchant seamen battled for their lives as well as their ship and its cargo, but pirates were unlikely to spare anyone who dared to resist them.

BATTLE REPORT

Fatal attack

In May 1722, the Italian pirate Matthew Luke attacked the English warship HMS *Launceston* in the dark. He thought it was a merchant ship—fatal mistake! The pirates were captured, taken to Jamaica, and hanged. Luke confessed to taking four British ships and murdering all of their crew. One of the pirates, a Spaniard, claimed to have slain 20 Englishmen with his own hands.

STOLEN TREASURE

Pirates pillaged ships for anything of value. Hoards of gold, silver, and jewels were the most prized of all booty. Almost as precious were colorful silks and spices, such as cloves, pepper, and nutmeg, from the Far East.

PRECIOUS CARGO

There are lots of stories of pirates keeping their treasure in chests, which they buried on remote islands. Treasure was often transported in chests, but in reality, pirates rarely buried their loot. They usually couldn't wait to enjoy their ill-gotten gains.

BURIED TREASURE

One pirate known to have buried his treasure was Captain William Kidd, a Scottish privateer. In 1698, Kidd captured the *Quedah Merchant* in the Indian Ocean, with its cargo of silk and other precious goods. On his journey back to North America, Kidd was accused of being a pirate. He hid some of his treasure by burying it on Gardiner's Island, and then claimed he was innocent. The booty was found and Kidd was hanged. Before his execution, Kidd said he buried another vast hoard somewhere in the "Indies." Treasure hunters have been looking for it ever since!

LOOT FOR LOADING

Some pirates raided coastal towns, taking anything they found, including casks of food and liquor. Here, in a scene from the movie *Aybolit-66*, stolen goods are piled high on a beach, ready for loading onto the pirates' ship.

FIGHTING TALK

Piracy's greatest hoard

In 1694, the English pirate Henry Every and his crew attacked a treasure ship belonging to the Grand Moghul of India. They took precious metals and gems worth an estimated $400 million in today's money. The loot made Every the richest pirate in the world, and it has been called the greatest hoard in the history of piracy.

PIRATE WOMEN

Throughout history, there have been women who sought adventure and fortune on the high seas. Women wielded swords and cutlasses alongside other pirates. Some even commanded their own pirate fleets.

PIRATE COMMANDER

Grace O'Malley, shown here as she may have looked, was the proud Irish commander of three pirate ships. The daughter of a sea captain, she became an expert sailor at a young age and gained a reputation as a fierce fighter.

FIGHTING TALK

Pirate meets queen

In 1593, Grace O'Malley's son and half-brother were taken captive by the English. Grace, now 63 years old, sailed to England to ask Queen Elizabeth I for their release. The queen agreed to meet her and was so impressed by this remarkable warrior that she granted all of Grace's requests and allowed her to continue her life of piracy!

PIRATES IN DISGUISE

In 1720, a pirate ship captained by the notorious "Calico Jack" Rackham was engaged in battle off the coast of Jamaica. Two of Rackham's crew were women dressed as men. With most of their shipmates below deck, Anne Bonny and Mary Read fought hard to defend the ship. The battle was fierce, but eventually, the crew was captured and condemned to death.

ANNE BONNY AND MARY READ

When Irishwoman Anne Bonny (left) fell in love with the pirate "Calico Jack" Rackham, she decided to join his crew. On board his ship, she found Mary Read. Disguised as a man, Read had served in the British Army before becoming a pirate.

ESCAPE FROM EXECUTION

Anne and Mary were both pregnant when captured, so they escaped execution. Anne managed to get away, and some say she had 10 children and lived to the age of 80. Mary died in prison, possibly during childbirth.

THE PIRATE KNIGHT

Sir Francis Drake was the first English sea captain to sail around the world and a pirate with royal approval! Before England's war with Spain (1585–1604), Drake stole Spanish treasure worth many millions in today's money.

GOING ASHORE

Francis Drake first tried his hand at piracy in 1572–73. Having sailed to Central America, he and his crew went ashore. They ambushed a mule train in Panama that was transporting Spanish treasure. They captured over 45,000 pounds (20,000 kg) of gold and silver, and made off with as much as they could carry.

GENTLEMAN PIRATE
Francis Drake (played here by Patrick McAlinney) was a hero to the English but a pirate to the Spanish.

ROYALLY REWARDED

Between 1577 and 1580, Drake made the second ever around-the-world voyage. On his way, with permission from Queen Elizabeth I, he plundered Spanish ships and bases. On his return, Elizabeth took a large share of the loot and gave Drake a knighthood!

THE GOLDEN HINDE
When it returned home in 1580, Drake's 22-gun ship was probably the richest ever to sail into a British port.

MAIN MAST
Drake's galleon had three masts. The main mast in the center was 92 feet (28 m) high.

SAIL
Drake's ship had five square sails; total sail area: 4,150 square feet (386 sq m).

HULL
The *Golden Hinde* had a wooden hull 102 feet (31 m) long and 22 feet (7 m) wide. It had a sailing speed of 9 knots (9 mph or 15 km/h).

COMBAT STATS

Around-the-world loot

- **From the first ship Drake attacked:** gold worth 25,000 Spanish dollars, worth about $11 million today
- **From the *Cacafuego* treasure ship:** 80 pounds (36 kg) of gold, 57,000 pounds (26,000 kg) of silver, 13 cases of coins, pearls, jewelry, precious stones
- **Drake's share:** from the whole voyage, money worth more than $15.5 million today
- **Crew's share:** from the whole voyage, money worth more than $12.4 million today shared between them
- **Queen's share:** enough to pay off all her debts and have money worth over $65 million today left over

From the Mediterranean to the Atlantic, the Pacific, and the Indian Ocean, pirates have plundered ships in all the world's seas. Some of the largest and most powerful pirate fleets operated in the waters of Southeast Asia.

CHEN ZUYI

In the fourteenth century, Chen Zuyi was the most feared pirate in Southeast Asia. With 5,000 men under his command, he terrorized traders in the Straits of Malacca (linking the Pacific and Indian Oceans) for many years. He was finally captured in 1407 by a Chinese voyager named Zheng He.

ZHENG HE—PIRATE DEFEATER

Zheng He was a mariner who utterly destroyed Chen Zuyi's pirate fleet. Chen was sent back to China for public execution.

28

PIRATE QUEEN

The largest pirate fleet of all time was led by a Chinese pirate named Ching Shih. With her vast "Red Flag Fleet" and many thousands of pirates under her control, she dominated the South China Sea in the early nineteenth century. She retired from piracy in 1810, when she accepted an **amnesty**. She negotiated **pardons** for most of her men, kept all of her fortune, and ran a gambling den until her death at the age of 69.

UNDEFEATED COMMANDER

The character Mistress Ching, seen here in the movie *Pirates of the Caribbean: At World's End*, was based on Ching Shih, perhaps the greatest pirate of all. A brilliant and ruthless commander, she remained undefeated against the Chinese, British, and Portuguese navies.

COMBAT STATS

Ching Shih's Red Flag Fleet

- **Location:** South China Sea
- **Active:** 1805-1810
- **Size of fleet:** over 1,800 ships
- **Number of pirates:** 70,000-80,000—over 17,000 directly under Ching Shih's command, the rest being made up of other pirate groups who worked with her fleet

GLOSSARY

amnesty an agreement by officials to take no action against someone who has committed an offense

bandit an outlaw or robber

bireme an ancient ship with two rows of oarsmen on each side

camouflage to disguise or cover up

cargo the goods carried on board a ship

cutlass a sword with a thick, curved blade

doubloon a Spanish gold coin

execution being put to death

flintlock a gun fired by a spark from a flint

frigate a small, fast warship

galleon a large sailing ship with three or more masts, used especially by Spain in the fifteenth to seventeenth centuries

gun port an opening in the side of a ship from which guns could be fired

hull the body of a ship

ill-gotten taken by illegal means

loot stolen goods

merchant ship a type of ship used for transporting goods for trade

missile an object that is fired from a weapon

musket an early form of rifle

navigator the sailor who directs the route of a ship

pardon a release from punishment

pieces of eight silver coins each worth one-eighth of a Spanish dollar

pistol a gun that could be held and fired with one hand

plunder to steal goods by force

rapier a sword with a thin, pointed blade

rigging the ropes that support a ship's masts and sails

tactic the way a plan, such as a battle plan, is carried out

trader a person who buys and sells goods

trigger the piece of metal that operates the firing mechanism in a gun

vessel a ship

FURTHER INFORMATION

Books

Lives of the Pirates: Swashbucklers, Scoundrels (Neighbors Beware!) by Kathleen Krull (Harcourt Children's Books, 2010)

Pirates by John Matthews (Carlton Books, 2011)

Pirates (Navigators) by Peter Chrisp (Kingfisher, 2011)

Sea Queens: Women Pirates Around the World by Jane Yolen (Charlesbridge Publishing, 2010)

Versus: Pirates by Richard Platt (Kingfisher, 2010)

Web Sites

America and the Barbary Pirates

http://memory.loc.gov/ammem/collections/jefferson_papers/mtjprece. html

In the late eighteenth century, President Thomas Jefferson dealt with America's first major foe: pirates. Read all about it from the Library of Congress collection.

A General History of the Pyrates

http://digital.lib.ecu.edu/historyfiction/item.aspx?id=joh

An online edition of an eighteenth-century book about pirates by Daniel Defoe, author of *Robinson Crusoe*.

Pirates in the Atlantic World

http://amhistory.si.edu/onthewater/exhibition/1_5.html

This fascinating Smithsonian site is part of its "On the Water" exhibit. It includes everything you wanted to know about the lives of famous pirates, a pirate's daily life, arsenal, and gear, plus the songs and stories that have immortalized them!

Index